Still Dancing

By

Jan Sargeant

Contents

Dedication

Dedicated to Ted Kennedy - my rock, my husband, my carer, and the man who taught my body and mind to sing again.

Acknowledgements

This would not have been possible without the support and encouragement of many people. You know who you are, and I thank you.

Thank you to the publishing team for helping me to realise this dream.

About the Author

Retired university lecturer Jan Sargeant lives in a small conservation village near Leeds with her husband, three cats and a dog. Her first novel, a comedy, will be published in 2023, and she was voted Writer of the Month by Spillwords readers in 2022. She is an Emeritus poetry editor for The Quiver. Jan was diagnosed with Parkinson's Disease in May 2016 and then, in 2022, with Giant Cell Arteritis. A successful artist as well as a published writer, Jan refuses to allow increasing disability to limit or define her.

Authors Note

Life deals you cards you never expected. You can't argue with a diagnosis of Parkinson's – it is what it is. It has a far-reaching impact on those diagnosed and those closest to them, who find themselves over time becoming carers as much as spouses, partners, daughters, and sons …This isn't a book of poems about Parkinson's, though. It's a book of poems about life, about love, challenge, loss, grief, anger, joy, change and dreams. Parkinson's will never limit my spirit, nor will I allow it to it define me. It is just one piece of a jigsaw, in a life enriched by all the people I'd never have met otherwise, by the creativity which now fills my life in both writing and painting.

Parkinson's changes lives, yes. It is a progressive and incurable disease which is disabling and degenerative, and it is the fastest-growing neurological condition in the UK. It is vicious, and it is remorseless. That's why profits from the sale of this book will go to support research into a cure.

I am enjoying the journey I've been making since May 2016, when I was diagnosed. It isn't what we imagined when my husband and I were discussing our future plans and dreams. So we created different plans and new dreams instead. Thank you to those people along the way who have taught me so much about playing the cards you're dealt instead of wishing for a different hand and those who have encouraged and supported me in new adventures.

Parkinson's in the UK: Stronger Together

The Quiver

Parkinson's UK

Parkinson's Art

Love Writing

Globe Soup

Lakeside Arts Group

Still dancing represents defiance, the refusal to be beaten or minimised by this condition. I'm a poet, an artist – I just happen to have Parkinson's.

Jan Sargeant

Tango on the terrace

Shall we take a quick step in the kitchen,
Jog a foxtrot across the lawns
Would you waltz with me through corridors
If I offered you my arms?
Could we dance the tarantella
Or beat a rumba into play,
Poke around with a polka
Before the orchestra fades away

Put some rhythm in my step
Pull my body hard to yours
Clasp your hands around my neck
Move in time towards my hips,
Let's tango on the terrace, dear,
And put your mouth
Against my lips

Warrior woman

You were going to be so many things
The soft touch of a new dawn,
A fingertip touching cheek
Nuzzling warm milky lips
Kissing sweet drips
From puckered mouth

Warrior woman,
Facing down dragons,
Laughing at scorn,
Striding across skies
Smashing through lies
Seeing Strength in a Mirror
Self-belief not disguise

I watched your blood flushed away,
One fat, smiling August day
Thought I'd rather die
But couldn't

Anaesthetised
When they scraped your brother away
"Cleaned me up", I heard a doctor say,
Wished I could die
But Didn't
4

I hear your voice in my dreams
Even today, watch you play,
See your skirts as they fly
Soothe your tears when you cry
Imagine the feel of you,
Taste the scent of you,
Know the touch of you
Ache with the loss of you

Lived a lifetime of love with you
Imagined an entire future with you,
Filled hours with hopes and dreams of you
In the forty short wonderful days, we knew
Together

I didn't see you there

Hello, old friend,
I didn't see you there
Grey faced uncertain edges
At the corners of a mind
Rounded by blurred optimism,
Vague shapes indistinct
From what might be true
And what might not
Will we know the difference,
Would we care?

Hello old friend,
Do you share
The invisibility of indecision,
Do you fear the lie
Hear it cry and then wonder why
It's plucking at your temples
Like a pizzicato string

Will you walk with me through shadows,
Or take my hand and lead,
Will you guide me to safety
Or stand and watch me bleed

I didn't see you this time

I didn't see you coming

But I see through your disguise

I see the way you look at me,

And hate the pity in your eyes

Grey faced blurs in discriminate skies

The pallid pastels of meaningless whys

Don't hide in the shadows

Of the past or the now,

Don't cloak yourself in darkness

Of a future that might never be

Don't huddle in the corners,

Stand up and let me see

Hello, old friend,

I didn't see you there....

Life in a tin

Whose memories fill boxes
With disappearing years,
The dissolving fears of
Torn wallpaper thoughts
Clutching at walls no longer there,

Whose memories are those,
Lying as spilt puddles, huddled
Drops of places and faces,
Seeping through spaces and
Cracks in floors no longer there

Photos and papers, an old sugar tin
Bought at a market, then opened on a whim,
Imagine finding a life hidden within
Old postcards thrown in a box
Unwritten stories of people lost,
Scraps of fabric, eyeless windows
The colander minds of forgotten years,
Half-baked days and burnt toast months

Derelict thoughts in a derelict mind
Clinging to unreality and scratching to find
Some sense of the person now left behind
In those boxes of memories

8

And torn wallpaper thoughts,
Scraps of a lifetime stuffed in a tin
The life of a stranger hidden within,
Whose memories fill boxes
With disappearing years

Origami tastes

I'm hanging on here
Wired up, strung out, paper fold shapes
Origami tastes,
Squeezed at the corners,
Pushed into place,
Jerking as hanged men
Splashing their feet,
Knowing there's a reason -
But not trying to compete;

Finger pressed creases
In a land of misshapes
Fog plaited memories,
Refuse to hang straight
Wired out, strung up,
We wait out our fate

Origami paper shapes
Folded through days,
Creased up, strung out as
A way through the haze

Hope

I bring you hope in a handful of fears
In the scent of dead violets
In the breath of a breeze
A moment of stillness, a pause in a line,
A twilight of years in pale rays of dusk-shine
The crepuscular glow before dawn in a sky
A question we all ask, and the need to know why

Don't measure change in fragments of time,
The space between then and what there is now
Hear the moan of the sea as it strokes across land
The grumble of rocks as they crumble to sand
Touch the space in the seconds
Between Hope and the Dream
Of who you might be, not who you have been

Silence speaks louder than words

In the fractured hours of still nights,
Murmuring minutes between
Dusk's ashes and a freshly mown morn,
Trickles of time tap at temples,
Scour eyes with smudged shadows
Of pale bruises, and it's then when
Silence speaks to me louder than words

Thoughts crawl from crevices in my brain,
Slither to mouth, coil as word shaped forms
Which pulse and quiver, hissing to be heard
But I trap them, bite them, swallow them whole
Spit out skin shaped husks
Which won't ever be shared because
Silences speak louder than any words

I'm digging through shadows,
Chopping at light, waiting for voices
To enter a long night where ciarascuro
Patterns flicker and lie, and monochrome
Mumbles cut through cardboard skies
I'm walking a map of muttering streets,
The stuttering retreats of imaginary lives
And listening to the silence,
Louder to me than words

12

Prayers, words and dreams

Prayer comes lightly to those
Who know the words but don't feel,
To those who crumble stock cube emotions,
And pass them off as real, while milk white
Confections masquerade, touching
Hands to psalm books, shaking
Dismissal at absent words on a page

Words come lightly to those
Who know what they should feel
But are numbed by fear, the slow freeze
Of ice in a brain splintering and gashing,
Slicing and slashing, an icepick smashing
Through crystalline dreams

Dreams come lightly to those
Who sit at the side, watching others
Risk failure, those who prefer to slide
Into the gap between desire
And choosing to decide,
The space between wanting
And the will to survive

Wipe me, wash me and wrap me

Wipe me, wash me and wrap me
In the brain fog exhaustion that rolls you
From one day to the next, the tender fingered
Devotion of medication you count out for me,
Dosette -box for me, hold out to me and
Some days mistake for me

Wipe me, wash me and wrap me
In old dreams, those we once knew,
Peeling memories of a universe away,
Stumbling, shuffling days and weeks
That now shiver and tremor as years,

Hold the cup to my lips, the crayon to my hand,
Mop the pee from the floor
Help me walk across a room
All this and so much more
You wipe my tears with your gentle smiles
Wash bubbles of laughter across my eyes
Wrap me in the songs we once knew,
The ones we used to sing,
And while we clear away the rubble of an old life,
We create the beginnings of something new

Don't tell me

Don't tell me what's safest,
What's best for me, don't tell me
What I need to do, when I need to be in bed,
If I need to be in bed, which bed I need to be in
But if you're not in that bed,
I do understand why

Don't tell me when I need to eat,
What I need to eat, how I need to eat
If eating this will be better than eating that
And don't tell me you're only thinking of me
When we both know you're scared

Don't tell others that I need to rest more
That cooking is too much now,
That a buffet is so much better
When you haven't a clue, or you'd say
Casserole or stew and we both know
You're scared, just like me

Don't tell me what's safest,
What to do, when and where
Let's just make it up
And take it from there

That time of night

Gets to that time of night
And your brain starts to fizz
And twirl with dance steps
Unchoreographed spontaneity
Shapeshifting patterns in a
Kaleidoscope of swirls
Desperate to breathe

Gets to that time of night
And your fingers twitch
And ache with images
Throbbing as seed pods
So swollen they must burst

Gets to that time of night
And your breaths quicken
In anticipation
Of the moment when
The paint splashes a page
With a heavy sigh
And words tremble
And shiver across a page

Some nights are hard

An hour whispers through a mind
Hardwired inside a brain
Tucked inside a body whose hand pulses
With an energy she doesn't own,
A hand she doesn't recognise,
And feet which only shuffle
When what she really wants is
To dance

A day whispers through a mind
Curling through the garden where
She'd heard the tremors of a robin's wings,
The urgent murmured sound of
A thousand beetles rattling
Before a flight which will shatter
Poisonous skies

Sleep now trickles in phrases
Punctuated by the sighs of seconds
Growing fainter, stumbling
And fumbling, howling frustration
At a moon which ceased to care years ago,
At a sun whose glare bleeds through eyes

October

I love the scent of wood fires
The burnishing of falling leaves
Pale, weak sunshine pushing
Slanting shadows across fields
The slow journey into autumn
The nip of a frost silvered breeze

I love the glow of lamps
Whispering down streets
The softness of curtains being
Drawn in softly fading light
The murmur of smoke
As it touches the night

October mists
The smell of heavy fruit
Dropped onto a ground hard to the touch
Chestnut husks bruised open
Lingering between leaves
And the geese fly south

Yesterday's song

Open lidded glimpses through eyes half closed
Colour shaped sounds of plaster smiles
Fragile as hoar frosted leaves

Do you remember the hands
Of a woman who sculpted cheeks
In a face smiling through time,
Whose laughter chuckled through a throat
Taut with loneliness

She wouldn't remember you now,
She crafts faces as ghosts
From a past, she never knew,
Strokes and moulds them,
Tender touch closes their eyes

No one moment when you say goodbye,
A single dot on the horizon as
A pinpoint of memory that never was
Memories with a music of their own,
Drumming their beat through blank staves
Strumming the chords of yesterday's song

To be warm

Cold eats into my bones
And I'm raw with white rime,
Raw white slivers
Frozen in time, trapped in the space
Between now and then,
Then and back when
I knew how it felt
To be warm

Ice trickling a path through veins,
Formaldehyde remains,
A fading flame of memory
In the frost of a numb brain
Of how it felt once
To be warm

I'm the cold ashes in the grate
The ice etched on a window pane
The chill in the air, the ghost of a breath,
I'm the cold, long wait

But sometimes, I can still remember
The glow of how it felt
To be warm

Gone

I am gone

Music

Lost in silences

Between breaths

In spaces

Between notes

In that moment

Of the second

Of the minute

Of the hour

Which rolled into days

Todays and tomorrows

Stretched beyond years

A melody shuddered

As the last chord frayed

Became a thousand echoes

And died...

In that nanosecond

When the last echo faded

Leaving sad silence

To fill the void,

In that moment,

That one, uncaptured,

Un-asked for, unwilling

Singular moment

Grief sobbed

Till its tears pooled

And pools became rivers,

And the rivers became seas,

Then the moon, tempted

By rolling tides,

Winked behind clouds

Nudged new dawns to break

Into long forgotten songs

Whose notes filled the spaces

Between the breaths

To fill the silences

And music

Filled the skies

Once again

I am returned

Letter from a person with Parkinson's

Dear Social Services, other helpful, supportive organisations, hospital workers, people standing behind me in a queue, people in pubs, friends and members of my family

I would like to explain that I'm not being difficult when:

1. *I need you to explain things more than once*

2. *I get lost easily*

3. *I'm slow filling in forms*

4. *I can't write properly*

5. *I forget my words*

6. *I get mixed up*

7. *I struggle to get money out of my purse*

8. *I can't do more than one thing at once*

9. *I take twice as long to do anything*

10. *I stumble and lose my balance without alcohol*

11. *I'm not being precious, but I do need to take my meds on time*

12. *I get as frustrated with myself as you do, but I'm not stupid*

So what else can I tell you?

1. *I've learned to live in the moment and just breathe*

2. *I've learned to rejoice in what I can do, not mourn what I can't*

3. I've learned to notice the small details which matter in a

life

4. I've learned the peace of acceptance without giving in

5. I've learned that when you strip away what I thought I

was, I am still me

Search for my words

Sometimes I find my words
Escaping from your mouth and
Wonder how they got there

Did I place them between your lips,
To be swallowed whole
Or drop them one by one,
Watch you swirl them around,
Taste them, savour their flavour,
Make them your own

Sometimes words stick in my throat,
Their congealed hard lumps
Filling cheeks with hollow space and
The stuttering trace of what I wanted to say
But couldn't spit it out before
The moment had gone,
Passed too fast, leaving me last
To hear my own words

When was it you took my words,
Shaped them, baked them, decorated
And staked them as your own;
And now, here I am, searching for my words,
Wondering where they're hiding,

Wondering when they became yours

Sometimes I sit in silence,
Watch as words dance into view,
Ask me now the question,
Did they come from me or you

Anchored by stillness

It was a hawk, not an eagle

As she scoured the sky

Eyes tuned to a feather's sound

Falling through air

As whispers to land

Soft on ground

It was a crow, not a raven -

Pitched as tar on a grey rooftop

Whose screeched demands

Were deafened by the song

Of one small blackbird

And it was one quiet voice

That spoke for the hundreds

In the clamour to be heard

The soft sibilant sounds

Anchored by the stillness

Thunderingly loud

Denial

Sitting by a window waiting for dawn,

Expectations shiver, seek

Warmth in the pale bonfire

Of what once were the vanities

Of a scalpel mind

Now searching to find

Colour in this washed out world of

Distortions, scratched contortions,

Monochrome stripped bare

Ciarascuro of shadows,

Images lost in translation,

An unfocused blur -

A new way of seeing

A kind of a dare - a gauntlet

Thrown down, the hope

Someone might care

Enough to want to look through my eyes

To see what's now there

Will you sit by this window with me,

Will you wait for the dawn

Protect as shadows choke me

Shelter me from this storm

Can we escape the distortions,

The scratched contortions,

The misshapes and the mistakes

The landscapes and the seascapes,

The wordscapes and the best

Of what was there before,

A camera obscura now obscured

By pin holes we never foresaw

Do androids dream

I asked Aunty Milly that once
But she'd never seen an android, she said,
Although she supposed they might
Aunty Milly was open to possibilities
Others never considered, and when
She died, and I knew Uncle Billy would
Leave us to join her soon - and he did

They say the world
Will whimper to the end,
Utter one last universal sob
Shuffle off its immortal coil and simply fade
Like tears in the rain when it's time to die

I saw hope today etched
In a grey face asking for chocolate,
I bought chocolate, but he'd gone,
No longer there, simply faded away
Or been shooed on? Difficult to say

I saw the murder of crows before
Charcoal wings pitched them high
Into a malevolent sky whose light was
Fading away like tears in the rain

When it's time to die, do we take our dreams
Do we wrap them as a talisman in tissue,
Hold them to our heart, or leave them as
Memories of who we once were before
We faded away

Uncle Billy said his dreams
And Milly's were kept in a drawer,
Tied together by a ribbon she'd worn
On their wedding day, and
No reason androids couldn't dream
All they needed was imagination

Do androids imagine
I asked the day after his funeral
Mother told me to stop wasting time
And to get on with the washing up

I think androids might dream
More than some people

Third shelf, kitchen cupboard on the left

Brittle smile painted on lips, fixed in place
On the face I wear outside,
The role play face, the daytime face
The one I wear for the folk I meet
Fumbling my way in the
Dusk to dawn rays,
The twilight mist which
Shrouds new days and
Suffocates my nights

The other I hide on the third shelf
In the kitchen cupboard on the left,
Behind a stash of things I never buy
Salvation in tinned peaches,
The canned calm of artichokes
Peanut buttered escape,
Piled high on a shelf to hide a face
I don't want others to see

Can I place my head on your shoulder
Can I sit and hold your hand,
If I were to show you that hidden face,
Would you understand
Would you point that face to the future
Or would you see it stashed back away

On the third shelf in the cupboard on the left
In the kitchen, night and day

Wordless response in lipstick
You slide towards my hand,
And I'm counting just how many smiles
Will need to be painted and fixed
Before anyone will want to understand

Third shelf, kitchen cupboard on the left,
That's where you will find me today
Hidden behind jars and bottles and cans,
Trying on different faces and
Whispering, "Go away."

This room doesn't want me

Controlled area, keep out
Strictly no admittance
Restricted area
Red circle guard with
White line keep out sign
A door that won't open
Without a code, they won't share
So I'm looking through a window
That isn't really there
At painted blossom
To help me not care
That this room doesn't want me
Not just yet, and not where
Cardboard's painted as concrete
To convince me to stay
Where a steel embrace
Lies in the grey metallic face -
A face with no eyes
Eyes lined with lies
Lies with no conscience
A face full of guise

And then the lunatics are in my head
And I'm singing their prayer
And the banging and clanging

34

The thumps and the groans lend
Descant to a chaos you feel in your bones
Your head is pinned to a cushion
Fixed firmly in place,
Your hand on a button they give you in case
You feel you might fall
They tell you no panic, you're simply to call
But you know that they're lying,
They're just feeding you dreams
There's no one to listen where
Walls can't hear your screams

Pages of data from which you emerge
Or figures to cover, to mask, and to submerge
Inside a room that never wanted you
Never wanted you that near
But for the time it allowed you,
Loved the taste of your fear

Women, eh

Difficult women
Women with a mind
Shroud in bandages,
Mummify then
Bury alive

She's still talking

Mummification not creation
More a living death
Stuff their mouths,
Cover their ears
Desecrate, suffocate

Is she talking now

Penetrate, denigrate,
Ridicule and patronise
Bind her and blind her
Stab deep into her eyes
Humiliate, castigate,
Pickle her brain in bile
Stitch her lips together
In a semblance of a smile

She's not talking now

Old woman thinking

Bishop takes queen, and pawns weep
Checkmate on a fading board,
Where sepia grasses wave
Over miles of yellowing memories

We're the dregs of an empty glass
Where drops of past horizons
Are licked by lips longing
To savour their taste
Just once more

And my eyes are crumbling
As my mind tries to recollect
When my past became the present
And the future lies only in my past

Back again

So you're back again
No dark corners this time
No hiding behind walls but
The full on glare of a spotlight turn,
No grey faced uncertainties,
Just stripped away seconds of
Monochrome minutes and
Stretched smears smelted
Into years of steel stares

Take back your shapes without forms
Your indistinct blurs,
The shivering quivers that crawl
Over rooftops, slide through the night,
Did you think I could want them,
Even imagine I might?

So you're back again
With ash dusted wrinkles - the chimes of old times -
The powdered confections
Of lies and disguise,
Your ratchet cold grin
As you twist at my sight
And the whispering muttering
Haunting long nights

Scrawl your shadow signature
On the splinters of the ice
That shatter any clarity with
That roll of a dice, I didn't know
I was rolling, that drumming tattoo
Of my fingers on my temple
As I watch now for you

And she sang ...

She loved the music of the wind

Whistling under doors

And she swore tides swelled

A symphony of their own,

She was convinced the clouds

Painted their own

Movement across skies,

Sketched in shadowy

Charcoal drifts of smoke

Teasing rooftops

Glowering above folds

Of moon-kissed fields.

She'd heard snowdrops gasp

White wonder stuttering frozen faces

Drowsy still with winter sleep,

Heard lilac hyacinths as they sigh

Their fragrance into a new dawn

When the breeze tiptoed in

To stroke her cheek, she knelt to

Smell warmed earth,

Felt the promise of new life

In her belly, circled it in one hand

And she sang

Nuclear

I'm glowing in my skin tonight
Fingertips flashing
Isotope burning
Imagination swirling
I'm nuclear
Watch me burn bridges
Splash skies with light
Cause confusion
Fuse delusion
I'm exploding here
You still want to fight?

Murals of my mind

I'm sitting in a corner of a room
Where laughter pools in puddles
And plastic hands line up
But not to applaud

Fading frescoes in layers of paint
On a wall from centuries ago,
Smudges of colours in a rhythm
Patched by motifs sliding into view,
A moment in a history,
A cell of time we never knew
So, for now, I'll stay sitting
In this corner of this room
Hold a mirror to its memories
Light a candle in the gloom

Can you see through the dust,
Through the patina of time
Will you stand by me, touch my hand,
Help me understand that
I'm sitting in a land
Where paint flakes layers from ancient walls,
Weeps through faded years,
Where echoes of forgotten calls
Still, stammer to be heard
In the murals of my mind

That's why I lie

Grey clouds ready to burst in
Floods of blood and tears
But you'll never hear me cry
Because the truth is the worst and
That's why I lie

Avoid truth - pretend it's the life
You wanted to live how it was planned to be;
Tunes with all the right notes but not the right order, see
I flinch at their discord, laugh through my grief,
Take my head in your hands and lay bare my disbelief
Comb your fingers through my fears
And then silence my cry.

Remember, truth is the worst and
That's why I lie.

Tell me what you see

When you look at me,

Do you see

Darkness filling my eyes,

The fading memories of

Sepia yesterdays

The shuffling shapes of

Abandoned todays

The muffled margins of tomorrows

Or just the shape-shifting ghosts

Of shadows in a sky of whys

When you look at me,

Do you see

Clouds laughing

Over moon-tipped fields

Or the frost-licked song

Of the wind in the trees

The pulse of a dawn

On the kiss of a breeze

Do you see

The unspoken thoughts

The words we didn't say,

The untouched canvas

Of an unlived day,

44

The lessons we learned

Along the way

The lessons we didn't

Tell me what you see

Sgraffito

Dark walls over layered graffiti
Verona drips and streaks
Her photos in deep, deep layers,
Marks and words
Scratches scores on
Rusted stencilled locks
Grey lampposts and black
Posters with razor blades

More layers of scraped through
Torn images of ripped memories
Ephemeral words fading through time
'Away with the mixer', mam said
Photos without context
Text without time

Accidental graffiti of passing lives
Lost memories like tears in the rain

Song of a Siren

I'm sitting in a cave
Where centuries of fossil stone
On hacked out walls are scratching at
Fingertips worn down by days
And laughing with the derision
Of those who know patience

Grape stained eye swollen thin
Straining to hear the murmurs within
Of the sigh of the tide, the call of a moon,
The rough hewn texture of the cave
Where I sit, a womb with no view,
A room with no sound,
A world with no colour,
A future to be found
In the grains of the rock
Of the walls which surround
With questions that only I ask -
The cave asks no questions,
Knows this, too will pass

I'm sitting in a cave where the walls call out
To yesterdays for hope, for hope for todays
As the slub of the sea, its inky wet gauze,
Might shape a new future,

Might open new doors

And the walls of the cave scratch
My hands and my feet
Green crystals of wisdom
Amidst the sea's beat
Be still and rest, be still and stay,
It's one day amongst many days

And this too will pass

Long shuffling night

Shivers of mortality creep-crawl
Shuffling long hours tonight
Sibilant sighs, hissing dreams
Chase, sleep away until you long for the day
And a glimmer of light in the dark

The gilded strength of sixty years
Lies shredded in a blanket of fears,
Wrapped shudders of shoulders,
Tattered tensions of arms,
And the tears you taste
Are sour with the memories of a woman
Who once strode winds and made planets fly

Shivers of mortality creep-crawl
Long hours tonight
And you lie, and you wait
Crying for the light
In the dark silence of one long night

This isn't anger ...

This isn't anger drumming through my fingers,
Hammering at twisted temples
It isn't anger clawing at my eyelids,
Peeled raw red pupils clenched close

It can't be anger because
There's a solace in the moonlight
Where trees play shadow shapes
With a night black as pearl,
Glowing hope through pain
Where clouds sleep over water and
As eyes ache, ears awake
To the sound of hope filling skies

Walk with me through tree-lined paths,
Listen to the rustlings and snufflings of early morning dew
Feel the beat of the drum of the pulse of a new hour,
Stretch out fragile wings, and in that moment of
Tender stillness, we breathe again as the spirit sings

This isn't anger drumming through my fingers,
Gnawing at my brain,
It can't be anger because
There's a solace in the moonlight,
And hope fills the skies

50

Transition

Dying is a verb, it wasn't ever a description
It takes energy and strength,
Cyanosis mottled cold hands
Clutching for warmth
From other hands

He's not there anymore
Though he left behind the skin still in his shape
And faint breaths which still fill the room,
And the imprint of a body still on a bed
But he's not there anymore,
At some point between then and now,
When all was still, he melted like snow

Small vessel circulation is shutting down now and will
enter deep sleep

Dirtier than I expected,
Nothing noble or gentle about this
Clinging to the uncomfortable
When the alternative is unknowable

Will enter a deep sleep, breathing rapidly changing pattern

No dignity in this bed
51

Haunted eyes dart from the ceiling

To floor where fear huddles

And arms search for arms

Breathing rapidly changes pattern, treat any distress

He's not there anymore

Left some time in the hours

Shifting between his memories and mine

In the shading minutes of purple to pink

His shadow slipped through a fissure

Seized a moment and went home

A foetus curls against a wall

As the light fades from the eyes

Treat any distress, comfort, no pain

As the light fades from the eyes, there is no pain

Only comfort, no pain,

Light fades from the eyes and no pain

He's not there any more

Transition complete

A new kind of Spring

When the birds stopped singing,
And the sun refused to rise,
The moon turned to the stars
Who turned to the clouds
Who scurried behind hills
And asked why

Why were there puddles
Splashed dry by winds
Whose orange bruises ached
Across indigo skies

We stood on the hillside
Plucked the stars out of clouds
Smoothed the moon with new tides
Eased the sun from its sleep
Hummed new tunes to the birds
And raised the curtain
On a new kind of Spring

Printed in Great Britain
by Amazon

28215985R00036